Australia's Environmental Issues

POLLUTION

REDBACK publishing

Redback Publishing
PO Box 357 Frenchs Forest NSW 2086
Australia

www.redbackpublishing.com.au
orders@redbackpublishing.com.au

978-1-925860-29-0

Author: Peter Turner
Editor: Michael Anderson
Proofer: Marianne Lindsell
Designer: Redback Publishing

Original illustrations © Redback Publishing 2019
Originated by Redback Publishing

Reprinted 2022
Printed and bound in Malaysia

Acknowledgements
Abbreviations: l—left, r—right, b—bottom, t—top, c—centre, m—middle
We would like to thank the following for permission to reproduce photographs: (Images © shutterstock) p20b IAEA experts at Fukushima Daiichi Nuclear Power Plant Unit 4, 2013 - IAEA imagebank.

Every effort has been made to contact copyright holders of any material reproduced in this book. Any omissions will be rectified in subsequent printings if notice is given to the publisher.

NATIONAL LIBRARY OF AUSTRALIA
A catalogue record for this book is available from the National Library of Australia

CONTENTS

WHAT IS POLLUTION?

Pollution is something that causes harm to an area of the natural environment, such as the air, soil or water. Pollution usually occurs when damaging substances, including chemicals or waste products, are introduced. The substances that cause pollution are called pollutants. Pollution can come from nature, but is mostly produced by humans. Pollution is a problem that requires rapid solutions, both within Australia and internationally, due to the growing human population and the increasing sizes of cities. Pollution can often be invisible, but just because we cannot see it does not mean that it is not causing damage to our health and to the planet.

Types of Pollution

There are many different types of pollution and ways that pollution can impact us, including:

- Harmful gases.
- Pollution can also be present in waterways, including rivers, oceans and even small creeks and streams.
- Chemicals and toxins can pollute soil, particularly around landfill sites where waste is dumped.
- Groundwater, polluted by toxins drifting downwards through the soil from landfill or other causes.
- Noise pollution.
- Light pollution.
- Pollution in outer space from old space shuttles and stations.

THE CAUSES OF POLLUTION

Pollution is often caused by the burning of fossil fuels, including coal, oil and gas, which are commonly used to provide energy and power. The main sources of air pollution are power stations, factories and motor vehicles. They produce a number of dangerous chemicals, including sulphur dioxide and nitrogen oxides, which are the main cause of a type of pollution known as acid rain. Emissions from cars and other vehicles also produce carbon monoxide and small toxic particles, including smoke.

THE EFFECTS OF POLLUTION

Pollution can cause many problems, including negative environmental impacts such as serious damage to plant and animal species. It can also cause immediate and long-term health effects in humans. Every time we breathe in, particularly in big cities, we inhale numerous pollutants that can irritate our throat and eyes, or cause asthma. Breathing in pollutants can also have long-term effects, such as damage to our lungs, the weakening of our immune system or even cancer. Certain pollutants can cause specific problems for people in the community who are vulnerable, such as small children and the elderly. Greenhouse gas pollution can even cause our climate to change over time.

AN INTERNATIONAL ISSUE

Pollution is a global problem because it does not respect national borders. Air and water pollution, in particular, can travel a long way from the original source to other countries. For example, toxic smog in China has impacted people in Japan and South Korea. Forest burnings in Indonesia impacted people elsewhere in Southeast Asia.

TEN DISTURBING FACTS ABOUT POLLUTION

01

In 2017 the results of a two-year study by The Lancet Commission on Pollution and Health were released and showed that pollution is responsible for an estimated 9 million premature deaths, and is the largest environmental cause of disease and death in the world today.

02

Air Pollution is responsible for causing 3,000 premature deaths in Australia each year.

03

Australia is the 5th largest producer of coal and the highest consumer of coal per capita, and as of August 2017, greenhouse gas emissions continue to increase.

04

Approximately 30% of agricultural land in Australia is severely degraded by salinity.

05

85% of Australian households put hazardous waste such as light bulbs and chemicals, in the rubbish bin.

06 A single plastic bag has a life expectancy of 1,000 years. Australians use 6.9 billion plastic bags per year. Only 3% of these are recycled.

07 Australians use 13 billion plastic drink containers annually.

08 1 million sea birds and over 100,000 marine mammals die each year because of plastics. 1 square kilometre of Australian ocean contains 4,000 fragments of plastic.

09 Every Australian resident uses an average of 341,000 litres of water per year.

10 Land pollution makes up 80% of all marine and freshwater pollution.

HISTORY OF POLLUTION

Pollution has not always been the significant global problem that it is today. However, there have always been natural sources of pollution, and over the centuries humans have also generated pollution that has sometimes proven deadly.

Natural Pollutants

In Australia, the most common example of natural pollution is smoke from bushfires, which contains ash, soot and carbon dioxide. In large quantities, bushfire smoke can make it difficult to breathe, and can even cause people caught up in it to suffocate.

Erupting volcanoes spew out lava, which is filled with toxic gasses. Gas emissions from volcanoes can also be a natural cause of acid rain. Hurricanes and cyclones can stir up toxins in the soil and carry them long distances before dumping them. They can also cause flooding, which picks up dangerous objects in the water and can also lead to illness from stagnant water that may remain after the flood has subsided. However, these are all unusual and occasional events, unlike pollution caused by humans, which often occurs on a daily basis over long periods.

THE INDUSTRIAL REVOLUTION

The beginning of many of today's pollution problems can be traced back to the Industrial Revolution in the 19th century. The discovery that coal could be burned to generate energy stimulated a massive change in human lives. However, it took a long time to realise that burning coal produced many toxins that polluted the atmosphere and were dangerous to human health.

The development of large machinery and enormous factories also produced great amounts of waste, and people living in industrial cities created problems of water contamination when they dumped their sewage water in the streets. In 1852, in London, this gave rise to what was called 'The Great Stink' – when large volumes of sewage in the streets led to overwhelming smells as well as an outbreak of waterborne diseases, including cholera.

MODERN CITIES

As cities have grown in size and become major centres of industry, commerce and population, they have also become major pollution centres. Numerous motor vehicles, factories and power plants produce huge quantities of pollutants in large cities every single day. The gases produced become concentrated in the atmosphere around the city and can have a negative affect on the health of people living there.

Some of the most polluted places on the planet are now large cities in developing countries. These cities have a significant amount of pollution being generated but very little regulation to minimise its dangers.

COUNTING DOWN THE TOP 10

According to the World Health Organization, the most polluted cities in the world are:

10. **Baoding, China**: Coal burning.

9. **Xingtai, China:** Steel production.

8. **Bamenda, Cameroon:** Deforestation.

7. **Raipur, India:** Sponge iron factories.

6. **Patna, India:** Industrial and vehicle.

5. **Al Jubail, Saudi Arabia:** The third largest producer of aluminium.

4. **Riyadh, Saudi Arabia:** Sandstorms, vehicle emissions and industrial waste.

3. **Allahabad, India:** Changing wind patterns, coal-burning power plants, vehicular emissions, and deforestation.

2. **Gwalior, India:** Burning garbage and fossil fuels.

1. **Zabol, Iran:** Dust storms than can damage lungs.

AIR POLLUTION

Air pollution is often invisible, but can still be very damaging, particularly over a long period of time. Every time we breathe in, pollutants can enter our body through air. This type of pollution can also travel long distances on air currents and can have an impact on people a long way from its source.

Major Air Pollutants

Some of the most common air pollutants are gases produced from the burning of fuel. Sulphur dioxide and nitrogen oxide are two common chemicals that are produced from electricity power plants and factories, as well as motor vehicles. These two chemicals cause a dangerous phenomenon known as acid rain. Carbon monoxide and lead, produced from the burning of fuel in vehicles, are also very dangerous, particularly in large cities. Lead has now been removed from petrol in many countries, but it is still common in developing countries and represents a major health threat.

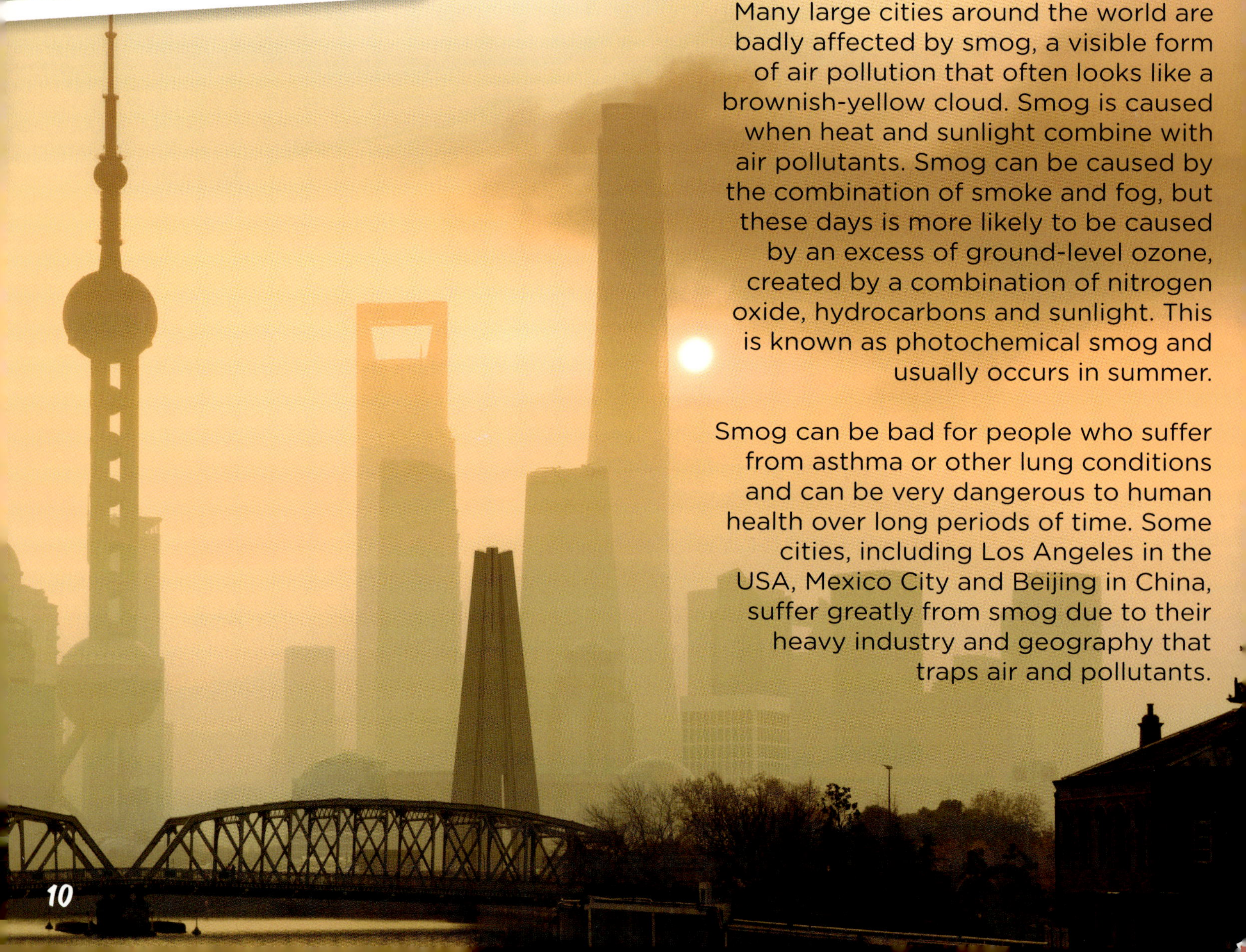

SMOG

Many large cities around the world are badly affected by smog, a visible form of air pollution that often looks like a brownish-yellow cloud. Smog is caused when heat and sunlight combine with air pollutants. Smog can be caused by the combination of smoke and fog, but these days is more likely to be caused by an excess of ground-level ozone, created by a combination of nitrogen oxide, hydrocarbons and sunlight. This is known as photochemical smog and usually occurs in summer.

Smog can be bad for people who suffer from asthma or other lung conditions and can be very dangerous to human health over long periods of time. Some cities, including Los Angeles in the USA, Mexico City and Beijing in China, suffer greatly from smog due to their heavy industry and geography that traps air and pollutants.

THE OZONE LAYER

While ozone at ground level is a pollutant that contributes to photochemical smog, it is an important layer of the upper atmosphere. There, it acts as a shield, helping to prevent the sun's harmful ultraviolet rays from reaching the Earth. The ozone layer is highly sensitive and has been partly destroyed by the effects of chlorofluorocarbons (CFCs), an artificial greenhouse gas used in aerosol cans, fridges, foam and some air conditioners. When CFCs rise in the atmosphere, they release the gases chlorine and bromine, which destroy ozone.

The first clear evidence of ozone depletion was in 1984, when scientists discovered that a large area over Antarctica had very little ozone at all, giving rise to the name the 'ozone hole'. It is not actually a hole, but represents a thinning of the ozone layer each year over Antarctica, South America and southern Australia. In 1989, an international treaty, the Montreal Protocol, was enforced to eliminate the use of CFCs, in order to reduce the damage to the ozone layer.

September 2017 marked the 30-year anniversary of the Montreal Protocol, now acknowledged as a success as the treaty is slowly but surely reversing the damage done to the ozone layer.

INDOOR AIR

Indoor air quality can sometimes be toxic. Exposure to high levels of pollutants from synthetic building materials, paints, carpets and even new furniture can be dangerous to human health.

New homes or renovations generally emit the most toxins, as toxic emissions from a product tend to decrease over time. Some new homes produce many times the maximum allowable limits of some indoor air pollutants. Regularly opening windows, using an indoor air filter, or even having indoor plants are ways to reduce the impact of indoor pollution on human health.

COMMON AIR POLLUTANTS

POLLUTANT	SOURCE	EFFECTS
LEAD	Exhaust fumes from vehicles using leaded petrol.	Lead can enter the lungs and blood stream, causing numerous illnesses.
OZONE GROUND-LEVEL	Formed when nitrogen oxides and hydrocarbons (released by motor vehicles and power stations) combine in sunny conditions.	A pollutant that forms photochemical smog and attacks the throat, damages the lungs and irritates the eyes.
CARBON MONOXIDE	Vehicle exhausts, burning fossil fuel.	Carbon Monoxide lowers the amount of oxygen in the body, resulting in tiredness and headaches. It can be lethal in high doses.
SULPHUR DIOXIDE	Coal-fired power stations and oil refineries.	Attacks the throat and lungs, causing breathing problems.
NITROUS OXIDES	Burning fossil fuels such as coal, petrol and gas.	Damages the throat and lungs.
PARTICLES	Vehicle emissions, bushfire smoke.	Damages throat and lungs, and causes breathing difficulties.

AUSTRALIA'S AIR POLLUTION HOTSPOTS

In Australia, 3,000 people die annually due to air pollution. In places like Mt Isa in Queensland, asthma mortality rates are 322 per cent higher than the rest of the state.

1. **Port Headland:** Pollution from iron ore dust.
2. **Mt Isa:** Pollution from copper, zinc and lead mines.
3. **Gladstone:** Coal and aluminium dust is a concern.
4. **Brisbane:** Nearly 9 million tonnes of coal is transport-ed through Brisbane's suburbs in uncovered trains.
5. **Hunter Valley:** Uncovered trains and coal are again a problem here, exceeding the national pollution standards 171 times.
6. **Morwell:** Coal fired power stations.
7. **Yarraville:** One street alone has 7,000 diesel trucks driving along it daily.
8. **Brooklyn:** Industrial estates give this suburb the worst air quality in Melbourne.
9. **Anglesea:** A coal mine and a power station contribute to pollution here.
10. **Port Pirie:** One of the biggest lead smelters in the world impacts the health of local children.

FRESHWATER POLLUTION

Litter is a common source of water pollution in Australia. However, like air pollution, water pollution can also be invisible. Rivers, lakes and streams may look dirty, but that does not mean they are polluted, as there may simply be suspended solids (like mud or silt) that need to settle. The reverse is also true; just because a waterway looks clean does not mean that it does not contain toxins that can be dangerous to human, animal and plant life.

Litter

Physical pollutants, litter including plastic bags, bottles, cans and even shopping trolleys, are highly visible forms of water pollution. When it rains, litter dropped in the streets is often carried into stormwater drains that commonly lead to nearby waterways. Litter not only makes waterways look ugly, but it can also affect water quality. It can block out sunlight and reduces the water's ability to produce oxygen which is vital for the survival of plant and animal life. Fish, birds and other animals can also get caught in litter and be seriously injured or killed.

CHEMICALS AND BACTERIA

Chemical pollutants can affect the amount of oxygen in a waterway, kill nutrients in the water or even change the colour, taste or temperature of a waterway. This can alter the water to favour certain animal and plant species, or it can have the effect of poisoning the entire waterway and everything in it.

Bacterial pollution, coming from poor sanitation or from untreated sewage released into waterways, can spread very quickly. This can cause serious diseases in those who drink the water or bathe in it. Contaminated water is a significant problem in many developing countries. A bacteria in water known as 'blue-green algae' can also cause problems, making it unsuitable for livestock or humans to drink.

Groundwater Pollution

Groundwater, which is the name given to water flowing deep below Earth's surface, exists underneath many parts of Australia. It can become polluted from a variety of sources. Toxins in soil, particularly near landfill, toxic waste sites or sewage treatment plants, can filter down into groundwater. Fertiliser and animal manure can also end up in groundwater. The water may travel long distances over time, taking pollution to larger water sources such as lakes, rivers or even the ocean.

Unsafe water causes the death of over a million people each year.

A child dies from a water related disease every 90 seconds.

884 million people worldwide live without access to safe water.

WATER THAT KILLS

When in Australia we take pure tap water for granted, elsewhere more than 1 million people die every year due to poor access to clean water. Many people in rural areas of developing countries must travel long distances every day to collect water for drinking and bathing. Their only water is often from polluted rivers, streams and wells. Many waterborne diseases can be spread through contaminated water, including typhoid, dysentery and cholera. Diarrhoea is often caused by contaminated water and is usually a minor annoyance in most places. However, in developing countries, it can lead to death.

Insects that breed in water can also spread diseases, including malaria and yellow fever. In 2016:

- 216 million people contracted malaria worldwide, an increase of 5 million cases from the previous year.
- 445,000 of those people died.
- 91 per cent of the deaths occurred in Africa.

MARINE POLLUTION

The seas and oceans of the Earth cover over 70 per cent of the planet, so they have an enormous influence on the global environment. Most substances dissolve or physically break down in water, but that is not the case with some forms of pollution. Ocean currents can also shift dangerous pollution hundreds of kilometres from its original source.

Strangling the Ocean

Up to 12.7 million tonnes of plastic waste is washed into the world's ocean each year. These plastics are wreaking havoc with marine animals. Plastic debris kills more than 1 million seabirds every year, as well as more than 100,000 marine mammals.

Most litter takes hundreds of years to break down, during which time it continues to pollute the ocean and damage marine life. Items such as plastic bags and rings from plastic 'six-packs' can entangle or get eaten by animals, including fish, marine birds, dolphins, whales and seals. Dumped litter also finds its way into the ocean through fresh waterways, adding to the problem.

MARINE MESS

MARINE ANIMALS OFTEN MISTAKE PLASTIC FOR JELLY FISH AND EAT IT, OR THEY BECOME ENTANGLED IN IT. THERE ARE NOW MORE THAN 46,000 PIECES OF PLASTIC FLOATING IN EVERY 2.5 SQUARE KILOMETRES OF THE OCEAN.

INDUSTRY AND AGRICULTURE

Many polluting heavy metals produced from factories and power plants end up being dumped or travelling through waterways to the ocean. Sewage that may be contaminated with toxic chemicals and bacteria is often pumped into the ocean. Pesticides and fertilisers from agriculture often end up in the ocean, causing toxicity, depleting oxygen levels and contributing to oceanic dead zones where little plant or animal life can survive.

OIL POLLUTION

We use oil for heating, cooking, making plastics and many other functions. But first it must be transported from where it is pumped out of the ground or ocean floor to where it is needed. Transportation is done over long ocean distances by oil tankers. Occasionally, these oil tankers have accidents, spilling large quantities of toxic oil directly into the ocean. However, most oil gets into marine water when tankers clean out their holds, which occurs on every ocean journey. Most of this oil ends up floating on the ocean surface and is carried on ocean currents. Any fish, plant or bird life it comes into contact with is coated with used oil. Some oil can sink and harm animal life on the sea floor with a toxic coating. It is very difficult and expensive to clean oil pollution from the ocean.

Montara Oil Spill

On 21 August 2009 the Montara wellhead platform drill rig owned by PTTEP Australasia suffered a well head accident, resulting in an oil slick in the ocean 110 miles wide at its smallest. It took around six weeks to clean up the oil spill, and marine life was seriously affected. The environmental impact has been ongoing. 15,000 Indonesian seaweed farmers have filed a $2 billion lawsuit against the company saying the oil spill destroyed their livelihood.

GREENHOUSE GAS POLLUTION

A very serious form of pollution, which has a direct impact on the atmosphere and the overall climate on Earth, is known as greenhouse gas pollution. Excessive amounts of certain atmospheric gases are directly contributing to a planetary condition called climate change, sometimes also known as global warming.

The Greenhouse Effect

The atmosphere above Earth is made up of a number of invisible gases, including carbon dioxide, methane, oxygen, water vapour and nitrogen. These gases trap heat within the atmosphere, keeping the planet warm and creating what is known as the greenhouse effect. When excessive amounts of certain gases are released into the atmosphere, the greenhouse effect is heightened and the planet becomes overheated.

In recent years, scientists have noticed that Earth's overall temperature has risen by nearly one degree, which may not seem like much, but small overall changes in just a few degrees can radically change many planetary conditions. While it is impossible to say by how much our overall climate will heat up and how drastic the changes to our environment will be, this global change in the climate is very worrying.

In Australia, the key drivers of emissions to 2030 are:

- Increased electricity demand linked to rising economic activity.
- Increases in transport activity linked to population growth.
- Increased livestock numbers in agriculture to satisfy international demand.

GREENHOUSE GAS EMISSIONS

Climate change is primarily caused by burning of fossil fuels, including coal, gas and oil, which all contain stored carbon dioxide which is released back into the atmosphere, increasing the greenhouse effect.

The biggest contributors to excessive greenhouse gas emissions are electricity generation, motor vehicle usage and industrial pollution. Agriculture generates carbon dioxide, as well as methane and nitrous oxide, two other potent greenhouse gases. Land clearing and deforestation release the carbon dioxide stored in the wood, another source of emissions.

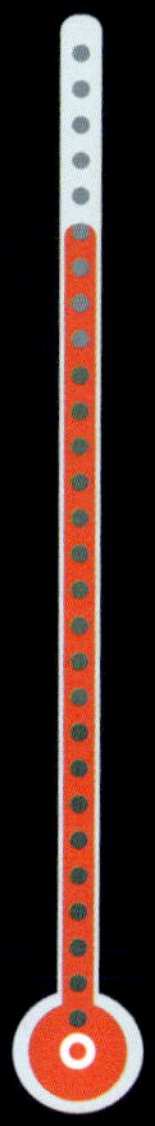

Sea level rise will redistribute shallow marine habitats around the coast, lead to saltwater intrusion into estuarine and freshwater coastal ecosystems and result in a loss of area of some habitats. This will be catastrophic for the animals that live in them.

Rising sea temperatures will also affect microscopic plankton, resulting in changes to the whole ocean eco system. All of Australia's ocean habitats, including the Great Barrier Reef will be impacted by these changes.

The rising temperatures also contribute to **coral bleaching**. Many reefs, including parts of the Great Barrier Reef are dying. This is a major problem as coral is part of a complex ecosystem, which provides shelter and food for many animals. The death of this coral impacts the whole food web, from tiny spawn and coral fish, to whale sharks.

EFFECTS OF CLIMATE CHANGE

Climate change is already causing some changes to the planet, but it is predicted to bring many more, including the melting of the polar ice caps, warming of the seas, heightened sea levels and an increase in extreme weather conditions, such as drought and flooding. It will change average temperatures in many locations around the world and will have an impact on farming, forests and many ecosystems.

It is likely that many plant and animal species will become extinct due to their inability to adapt to the changing climate. In Australia, we can expect less rainfall but stronger rain when it does come, along with more hot days and an increase in extreme weather events such as floods, cyclones and heatwaves.

These events could disrupt the normal cycle of variability to which animals and plants have adapted. Increased emissions of CO_2 to the atmosphere are partly absorbed by oceans, which increases the acidity of ocean waters and changes the physiology of marine organisms.

NUCLEAR WASTE

The process of generating nuclear power produces one of the most toxic pollutants on the planet - radioactive waste. It can cause serious disease and even death in humans and animals, as well as major environmental damage. Radioactive waste must be securely stored in order to minimize the dangers, but it also remains highly toxic for more than 10,000 years. Storage methods must therefore consider the safety of both current and future generations of humanity. Radioactive waste is usually buried deep beneath the ground or the ocean.

Fukishima

In March 2011, a massive earthquake in Japan triggered a devastating tsunami. The tsunami disabled the power supply and cooling of three Fukushima Daiichi reactors, causing a nuclear accident. There is much debate about the official information provided to the public about the ongoing health and environmental impact this accident had. The official line is that there have been no changes in radiation levels, which remain safe. Many researchers refute this, stating there are not only high levels of radiation in Japan, but the ocean too has been affected.

CHERNOBYL

In 1986, there was an explosion at the nuclear power plant at Chernobyl, Ukraine, in central Eastern Europe. The official death toll was 3,600 people, but the number of humans and animals affected was much higher. A cloud of dangerous radioactive pollution travelled more than 3,000 kilometres from Chernobyl across Europe, as far as Iceland and Greece. The pollution caused agricultural contamination for up to two years after the accident in many European locations, including Scandinavia and Britain. A wide variety of agricultural crops and grazing animals were found to have absorbed large amounts of radioactivity, which made them unsuitable for human consumption.

Today, more than 20 years later, some European land is still contaminated. A number of international laws have been brought in to better control pollution and reduce its impact, but still much more needs to be done.

OTHER TYPES OF POLLUTION

While pollutants in the air and water are most common, there are many other types of pollution that are not immediately visible but have a negative impact on our lives and environment.

Soil Pollution

Toxins and heavy metals, including cadmium and chromium (found in batteries), lead, zinc, arsenic and benzene, can contaminate soil. Before people realised how dangerous toxic waste was, they would often bury it in the soil to get rid of it. But this creates ongoing problems in the surrounding area.

Sometimes, animals eat plants that have absorbed the toxins, and then people eat the animal and become sick. Often, plants will not even grow, due to high levels of toxins in the soil. People who have lived near landfill dumps or toxic waste sites also have higher levels of asthma and other diseases. Eventually, toxins can seep down through the soil and contaminate groundwater, creating water pollution.

NOISE POLLUTION

Noise pollution is a form of air pollution that can not only be very unpleasant but can also cause stress and illness, lasting damage to our hearing and even heart disease.

People living near airports, main roads and freeways, and construction sites commonly experience noise pollution. Noise pollution can also come from nightclubs and concerts, or from burglar alarms installed in cars or houses.

Noise is measured in decibels. Sounds up to 10 decibels are almost impossible for us to hear, but a level of 140 decibels (that of a powerful drill) is considered to be dangerous to human hearing.

LIGHT POLLUTION

This is a highly visible form of pollution, caused by an excessive amount of light. It is often produced at night in large cities, but can also be found indoors, where excessive lighting of an area may lead to worker stress and poor health.

Sources of light pollution include advertising billboards, streetlights, office building lights and other unnecessary indoor and outdoor lighting. It can disrupt the natural routines of animals and cause negative health effects in humans. It can generate a nightly glow in the skin in very large cities, and can prevent city dwellers from ever seeing the stars. Light pollution also produces greater amounts of other forms of pollution, as the energy needed to keep the excessive lights running generates polluting greenhouse gases.

POLLUTION IN SPACE

Humans have been exploring outer space and launching satellites into orbit around Earth since late 1950s. Most of these satellites are still in space, even though they may no longer be functioning. Many space shuttles eject part of their framework during flight, and these parts are still orbiting the Earth.

It is estimated that there are more than 500,000 pieces of space debris, or junk, currently being tracked. They can easily collide with one another, breaking apart and creating smaller pieces of space junk. They can cause problems for other satellites or space shuttles, which would be damaged or even destroyed if they collided with space junk. The International Space Station, which orbits the planet, has a special shield to protect it from floating space junk.

AGRICULTURE AND POLLUTION

Agriculture, which is the growing of crops and raising animals to provide food, can also produce many dangerous forms of pollution in the air, ground and waterways. Agricultural pollution is often not immediately obvious, but may build up over time.

Chemical Usage

Farmers use a huge array of chemicals, including fertilisers to help crops grow, pesticides to kill insects and other small creatures that may eat the crops, and herbicides to kill weeds. While these chemicals may perform an important function in the short term, they also contain numerous toxic chemicals, such as phosphates and nitrates, which cause significant damage to plant, animal and even human life in the long term. The chemicals soak into the soil, depleting it of nutrients over time and filter down to pollute groundwater. Or they wash off the land to pollute rivers and streams. Manure from farm animals that eat crops sprayed with chemicals is also polluted and may end up in the soil or waterways, increasing the chemical concentration.

METHANE AND NITROUS OXIDE

Agriculture also contributes to greenhouse gas pollution, producing 16 per cent of Australia's yearly emissions, primarily with two gases. Nitrous oxide is produced over time when the chemicals that farmers use on their crops deplete the soil of nitrogen, which is released into the air as nitrous oxide.

Methane is produced from grazing animals, mostly cows and sheep, which release methane as they digest their food. It is also released from their manure. Currently, methane accounts for 10 per cent of Australia's total greenhouse gas pollution.

DEAD ZONES

Excessive chemical usage has created a number of oceanic dead zones, where marine life struggles to survive. The nitrogen and chemical run-off from farms eventually flows through to the ocean and creates what is known as a 'hypoxic zone' where there are low oxygen levels in the water.

The largest dead zones occurs in the Gulf of Mexico, where chemicals from hundreds of farms in the southern USA have washed down the Mississippi River and into the Gulf over the past 60 years. This has created an area of ocean of 17,000 square kilometres in which very little plant and animal life can survive.

THE GLOBAL IMPACT OF DDT

The chemical dichloro-diphenyl-tricholoroethane (DDT) is an insecticide that was commonly used from the 1950s onwards. It was sprayed on crops to kill bugs, but was also used to control mosquitoes that caused malaria in tropical countries. DDT breaks down very slowly and remains in the environment for a long time, making its way up the food chain, stored in the fat cells of animals. It causes long-term damage to animal life, particularly birds, and is also known to be highly toxic to marine life. The impact of DDT on humans is widely debated, but it is believed to increase the risk of cancer and other common diseases.

There is now a worldwide ban on the agricultural use of DDT and it has been completely banned in Australia since 1997. However, it is still used in some developing countries to control malaria. Despite the ban, traces of DDT can be found in many humans on the planet (it gets passed down through breast milk) and it has even been found in Antarctic penguins.

INDUSTRIAL POLLUTION

Industrial sources, including coal, gas and nuclear power stations, as well as factories, produce a number of dangerous pollutants. The environmental impacts are greatest close to the original site of the pollution, but there may also be long-reaching effects, such as serious marine pollution.

The burning of fossil fuels, such as coal and gas, produces carbon dioxide and methane, as well as other chemical pollutants, including sulphur, nitrogen oxides, ammonia, hydrocarbons and more. Some industries also produce toxic waste, which can pollute soil and groundwater with heavy metals, including mercury, lead and dioxins. Fish ingest these toxins, and the larger or more long-lived they are, the more the toxins build up in their fat cells. When humans eat these large fish, including tuna, shark and orange roughey, we also ingest the toxins, which are then stored in our own fat cells. It can be damaging to human health if we eat large quantities of these fish.

TRANSPORT AND POLLUTION

Motorised transport is one of the main contributors to pollution in global society. Transport is the third largest source of emissions in Australia. Cars, trucks, buses, trains, ships and even aeroplanes all produce pollutants. Most modes of transport produce carbon dioxide, which is a polluting greenhouse gas, but they also produce many other pollution particles that are dangerous to human health.

Motor Vehicles

As of 2017, Australia has over 18.8 million vehicles on the road, powered by petrol, diesel or liquid petroleum gas (LPG), each of which produces a number of toxic particles every time they are driven, contributing to the country's greenhouse gas emissions. They also produce a number of other dangerous air pollutants, including sulphur dioxide, nitrogen oxide, carbon monoxide, and benzene. More drivers are choosing diesel vehicles. Diesel fuel also produces soot, which is a dark cloud of exhaust fumes containing dangerous particles. Not only are these toxins bad for human health, but they also contribute to photochemical smog, reducing visibility in cities and affecting lungs.

Australia has one of the world's most lenient sulphur standards for petrol, which is 15 times the limit allowed in the European Union, Japan and the US. It's three times what's allowed in Brazil and China.

CLEANER CARS

The hybrid car, which produces half the pollution of the average car, is now common, but the future may reside with the electric car, which has no exhaust fumes and produces no pollution whatsoever. The electric car runs on an electric battery that usually needs to be plugged into the electricity grid overnight to recharge. Electric cars could drastically reduce the amount of pollution produced by cars and decrease pollution problems in large cities.

WHAT CAN WE DO?

There are a number of ways that everyone can help to reduce the amount of pollution in society. The choices we make each day do make a difference and have an impact on air, soil and water pollution.

Reduce Car Usage

Since motor vehicle emissions are one of the most significant sources of airborne pollution, we can help to reduce emissions of sulphur dioxide and nitrogen oxide, as well as a number of other toxic pollutants, each time we choose not to use the car. Walking or riding a bicycle produces no pollution whatsoever. The more we can convince our family to give the car a miss and encourage others to do the same, the better.

SWITCH OFF

By turning off light switches, televisions and other electrical goods when we are not using them, we will reduce pollution from coal-fired power plants.

By choosing renewable energy to power our homes through the Green Power scheme, we can also reduce greenhouse pollution. This government-run scheme allows households to choose renewable energy - usually solar or wind energy - by paying a small premium above the standard electricity rates. Green power is available to all Australian households and by choosing it we can reduce our dependence upon polluting coal as an energy source.

DON'T BE A LITTERBUG

Litter makes a substantial contribution to the pollution of our waterways and soil, so the less there is of it, the better. Do not litter, and encourage others to take home their trash, not to dump it on the streets. Get involved in Clean Up Australia Day each year, and help remove litter from your local government area.

RECYCLE

The more we can recycle products, the fewer new products need to be made and the less emissions will be generated in making them. To make a new plastic, glass or aluminium product consumes significantly more resources and produces a great deal more pollution than to recycle the same products. Buying items second-hand and making sure our old household items are given away to charity or someone who needs them helps to reduce the need to manufacture new products.

GO NATURAL

Consider all the chemicals in all the many products that wash down our drains every day. Many washing detergents, hair shampoos and conditioners contain phosphorous and other chemicals that increase the toxicity of rivers and waterways, causing pollution problems. Ask your parents to use environmentally friendly cleaning products in the house and in washing machines. Used chemicals, particularly motor oil and paint, should never be poured down the drain as they get into waterways and cause problems. The more we can use natural products in our house and ourselves, the greater the reduction in pollution getting into our waterways to affect plant and marine animal life.

RENEWABLE ENERGY

Power generation is a major contributor to air pollution through toxins and greenhouse gases. So it makes sense to look towards alternative options to provide our energy needs. A small portion of our electricity needs is currently supplied from renewable resources, including solar (the sun), wind and even waste in landfills. These energy sources have low running costs, do not deplete fossil fuels and do not produce pollution during their running. However, as they are currently more expensive to set up than traditional power sources such as coal, they are still not commonly used.

The Australian Government aims to make renewable energy a source of at least 20 per cent of our energy needs by 2020.

AUSTRALIAN LAWS

Many Australian pollution laws are state-based, rather than national. However, an agreement between the states and territories and the Australian government in 1992 led to the development of the National Environment Protection Council. This body is dedicated to giving Australians protection from air, water, soil and noise pollution wherever they live. The Council develops national objectives for protecting or managing certain environmental pollutants, and the states and territories are then responsible for developing laws to implement them. The Council has been responsible for controlling diesel vehicle emissions, controlling air toxins, managing contaminated land sites, identifying and transporting hazardous waste, and maintaining a national database of pollutants.

The Environment Protection and Biodiversity Conservation Act 1999 (the EPBC Act) is the Australian Government's central piece of environmental legislation. It provides a legal framework to protect and manage nationally and internationally important flora, fauna, ecological communities and heritage places.

INTERNATIONAL LAWS

Over the past 30 years, however, some major international treaties have been signed to combat the effects of particular problems, including ozone depletion and global warming. One of the most successful international agreements to date is the Montreal Protocol on Substances that Deplete the Ozone Layer, which has been successful in removing the use of CFCs from developed countries. Further, The Kyoto Protocol is the first international treaty to focus on reducing greenhouse gas pollution to combat human-generated climate change.

The EPBC Act oversees issues affecting:

- **World heritage sites**
- **National heritage sites**
- **Wetlands**
- **Threatened species and ecological communities**
- **Migratory species**
- **Nuclear actions, and**
- **Commonwealth marine areas.**

GLOSSARY

atmosphere - the cloud of gases that surrounds the planet and protects us from ultraviolet radiation, while also trapping some sunlight and making it suitable for life

carbon dioxide - a greenhouse gas produced by burning fossil fuels

carbon monoxide - a toxic gas that comes mainly from car exhausts

chlorofluorocarbon (CFC) - an artificial greenhouse gas used in aerosol cans, fridges, foam and some air conditioners, which can destroy the ozone layer

climate change - the process by which the overall climate varies between one temperature and a new average temperature

contaminate - to make something impure or polluted by mixing harmful impurities into it

decibels - a unit of measurement used to measure noise levels

deforestation - the chopping down of forests, usually to produce wood or to provide land for human needs

dioxins - human-made chemicals that are the by-products of manufacturing processes and are toxic

fossil fuels - ancient fossils from plants and animals that died millions of years ago, including coal, oil and gas, which when burned release greenhouse gases

global warming - an increase in the overall climate of the planet caused by the release of excessive greenhouse gases into the atmosphere

greenhouse gases - invisible gases including carbon dioxide, methane, nitrous oxide and ozone, which are part of the atmosphere and function by trapping heat from the sun

groundwater - water flowing deep beneath the Earth's surface

landfill - a large pit dug into the ground where waste is buried

litter - food waste, packaging and other trash left in public places

methane - a greenhouse gas that is emitted from the belching of animals including cows and sheep, landfill sites and even from the natural gas that we use in our home

non-renewable - resources including water, minerals and fossil fuels that were created millions of years ago and will eventually run out

ozone layer - a layer of the atmosphere where the gas ozone provides a protective layer that shields the Earth from ultraviolet radiation

photochemical smog - visible air pollution caused by nitrogen oxides and hydrocarbons reacting in the presence of sunlight

pollution - something that cause harm to the air, soil or water by introducing damaging substances, such as chemicals or waste products

pollutants - substances that cause pollution.

recycle - to process waste material so that it can be used again

renewable resources - resources that are plentiful and will never run out, such as the sun and wind

sewage waste - water containing toxins from toilets and drains

smog - a visible form of air pollution where heat and sunlight combine with air pollutants, such as smoke or chemicals

sulphur dioxide - a polluting gas that is produced by burning coal and refining oil and gas

INDEX

FURTHER INFORMATION

Using the Internet

Explore the internet to find out more about topics discussed in this book. Use a search engine, and type in keywords like 'pollution', 'global warming' and the names of people, places and events you are interested in.